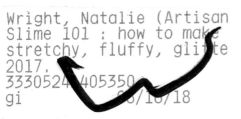

Slime 101

How to Make
Stretchy, Fluffy, Glittery & Colorful Slime!

Natalie Wright

Dover Publications, Inc.
Mineola, New York

CONTENTS

Bibliographical Note

Slime 101: How to Make Stretchy, Fluffy, Glittery & Colorful Slime!
is a new work, first published by Dover Publications, Inc., in 2017.

International Standard Book Number

ISBN-13: 978-0-486-82091-0
ISBN-10: 0-486-82091-2

Manufactured in the United States by LSC Communications
82091203   2017
www.doverpublications.com

INTRODUCTION

After writing this book, I can definitely say that I have been slimed…on multiple occasions. This has been one of the most fun projects I have ever worked on. As a mom of four kids, I had plenty of helpers! My family had such a great time spending hours in our little Kentucky kitchen testing out these recipes. We quickly became the "slime house" in our neighborhood, and I found myself buying plastic storage containers in bulk so kids could start taking it home. We may have also contributed to the glue shortage in the Lexington, Kentucky, area!

These recipes have been tested backwards and forwards, and I am proud to say we have compiled the most fun and easy recipes you will find. From textured slime to the ever-puzzling Oobleck, there is sure to be a recipe for everyone!

A couple of tips from a crafty mom

Depending on the climate, slime will last up to several months if stored in an airtight container. Be sure to have kids wash their hands both before AND after play. Slime can easily harbor bacteria, so throw it out if lots of hands play with a single recipe.

For little ones that are sensitive to textures, use rubber gloves or popsicle sticks so they don't feel pressure to directly touch any goo. My son has autism, and he found that a rolling pin was the best way to first dive in. Before we knew it, he was touching and squishing along with the rest of us!

There are several different slime recipes in this book, so check ingredients carefully. Excessive exposure to any ingredient can cause rashes or an allergic reaction in some children. I have chosen not to include Borax in my recipes, but we have safely made and played with it many times at home. The first time you make slime, watch your children closely. Never, ever, let children ingest slime.

Slime can be incorporated into playtime, educational time, outdoor time, and even on the go! It makes a great gift, and a fun party favor, too. Have fun creating these recipes together, and don't be afraid to get your hands dirty alongside your little ones!

SEQUIN SLIME

HERE'S WHAT YOU NEED:

5 oz. clear school glue
Contact lens solution
3 tbsp. sequins
1 tsp. baking soda
Small mixing bowl
Mixing spoon

STEP 1: Gather supplies. Plastic sequins can be found in a variety of shapes and colors at your local craft store. Choose sequins with rounded edges for ideal play.

STEP 2: Pour 5 oz. clear school glue into a small mixing bowl.

STEP 3: Slowly mix in 1 tsp. of baking soda.

STEP 4: Add up to 3 tbsp. of sequins in various colors. Stir together.

STEP 5: Slowly add ½ tsp. of contact lens solution one drop at a time while mixing together.

STEP 6: Continue to add contact lens solution until mixture is stretchy, but no longer sticky.

GLITTER SLIME

HERE'S WHAT YOU NEED:

5 oz. clear school glue
½ cup liquid starch
1 tbsp. glitter
3-4 drops food coloring
Spatula or mixing spoon
Large mixing bowl

STEP 1: Gather supplies. You can use a fine or chunky glitter, just be careful to avoid glass glitters that may cause scratches on the skin.

STEP 2: Pour 5 oz. clear school glue into a large mixing bowl. Add 3-4 drops of food coloring.

STEP 3: Sprinkle in 1 tbsp. of colorful glitter.

STEP 4: Slowly mix all ingredients together until slime forms.

STEP 5: Add additional glitter if needed. If slime is too sticky, add a few more drops of liquid starch.

STEP 6: Let slime rest for 2-3 minutes to fully set before play.

RAINBOW SLIME

HERE'S WHAT YOU NEED:

10 oz. clear school glue
1 cup liquid starch
6 plastic drinking cups
Food coloring in a rainbow
    of colors
Mixing whisks or spoons

STEP 1: Gather supplies. Plastic cups are a great way to mix smaller batches of slime!

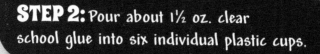

STEP 2: Pour about 1½ oz. clear school glue into six individual plastic cups.

STEP 3: Add 2-3 drops of food coloring to each cup. Set up your rainbow by creating a different color in each cup.

STEP 4: Mix 1:1 with liquid starch in each cup, one at a time, forming the slime until it is firm. If slime is sticky, add a few more drops of liquid starch.

STEP 5: Let slime rest for 2-3 minutes.

STEP 6: Align colors to create a rainbow, mix, and enjoy!

TEXTURED SLIME

HERE'S WHAT YOU NEED:

4 oz. white school glue
½ cup liquid starch
Food coloring
Mixing spoon
I cup polypropylene beads
Medium mixing bowl

STEP 1: Gather supplies. Polypropylene beads can be found in regular and micro sizes in the fabric and sewing section of your local craft store.

School Glue

Safe, Non-Toxic
4 Fl. Oz. WARNING:
(118 mL)

STEP 2: In a medium mixing bowl, mix 4 oz. white school glue with 2-3 drops of food coloring.

STEP 3: Add polypropylene beads and mix thoroughly.

STEP 4: Slowly add liquid starch to mixture, stirring until slime starts to form. If slime is sticky, add a few more drops of liquid starch.

STEP 5: Let slime rest for 2-3 minutes before play.

STEP 6: Enjoy! Textured slime works best when polypropylene beads are added before liquid starch. Do not add additional beads afterward, since they will have a difficult time sticking to the mixture.

GLOW-IN-THE-DARK SLIME

HERE'S WHAT YOU NEED:

- 4 oz. white school glue
- ½ cup liquid starch
- 2 tbsp. glow-in-the-dark craft paint
- Mixing spoon
- Medium mixing bowl

STEP 1: Gather supplies. Glow-in-the-dark craft paint can have a very light tint to it, so you may need to add neon yellow craft paint, depending on the brand.

STEP 2: Pour 4 oz. of white school glue into medium mixing bowl.

STEP 3: Add 2 tbsp. of glow-in-the-dark craft paint.

STEP 4: Mix glue and paint thoroughly.

STEP 5: Slowly add ½ cup liquid starch. Mix until slime has formed. If slime is sticky, add a few more drops of liquid starch.

STEP 6: Let slime rest for 2-3 minutes before play. Place slime in direct sunlight or lamp light for 2-3 hours for maximum glow.

CHALKBOARD SLIME

HERE'S WHAT YOU NEED:

4 oz. white school glue
Contact lens solution
1 tsp. baking soda
2 tbsp. black chalkboard paint
Medium mixing bowl
Mixing spoon
Chalkboard marker

STEP 1: Gather supplies. Chalkboard markers come in a variety of colors!

STEP 2: Pour 4 oz. white school glue into a medium mixing bowl. Add 2 tbsp. of black chalkboard paint. Mix thoroughly.

25

STEP 3: Slowly stir in 1 tsp. baking soda. Mix until baking soda has completely dissolved.

STEP 4: Slowly add ½ tsp. of contact lens solution one drop at a time while mixing together.

STEP 5: Continue to add contact lens solution until mixture is stretchy, but no longer sticky.

STEP 6: Prime chalkboard marker, and lightly draw on chalkboard slime surface. Knead slime to draw a new pattern or design.

METALLIC SLIME

HERE'S WHAT YOU NEED:

5 oz. clear school glue
½ cup liquid starch
1-3 tbsp. metallic craft paint
    in various colors
Plastic drinking cups
Mixing spoons

STEP 1: Gather supplies. Try to find a metallic craft paint that is high in sheen and pigment.

STEP 2: To make three different colors of metallic slime, pour bottle of clear school glue into even amounts in three plastic cups.

STEP 3: In each cup add 1 tbsp. of a different metallic paint. Mix well.

2 CUPS
1½
1 CUP
½
500ml
400
300
200
100

STEP 4: Slowly add equal amounts of liquid starch into each cup, stirring as you go.

STEP 5: Once slime has formed, let it rest for 2-3 minutes.

STEP 6: Mix and twist multiple colors together for a cool metallic effect!

BUBBLE SLIME

HERE'S WHAT YOU NEED:

4 oz. white school glue
½ cup liquid starch
Food coloring
Large mixing bowl
Mixing spoon
Plastic straws

STEP 1: Gather ingredients. Try straws in various sizes for different bubble effects!

STEP 2: Pour 4 oz. white school glue into a large mixing bowl.

STEP 3: Add liquid starch and 3-4 drops of food coloring.

STEP 4: Mix thoroughly until slime forms. If slime is sticky, add a few more drops of liquid starch.

STEP 5: Let slime rest 2-3 minutes before play.

STEP 6: Wrap a small amount of slime around the bottom of a straw. Gently blow to create bubbles. It may take a few tries to get it right!

NEON SLIME

HERE'S WHAT YOU NEED:

4 oz. white school glue
½ cup liquid starch
Neon food coloring
Large mixing bowl
Mixing spoon

STEP 1: Gather supplies. You can use neon food coloring or neon craft paint for this project.

STEP 2: Pour 4 oz. white school glue into a large mixing bowl.

STEP 3: Add 3-4 drops neon food coloring.

STEP 4: Pour ½ cup liquid starch into glue mixture.

STEP 5: Mix thoroughly. If slime is sticky, add a few more drops of liquid starch. Add additional food coloring if needed.

STEP 6: Repeat recipe to make as many neon colors as you like!

STRESS BALL SLIME

HERE'S WHAT YOU NEED:

5 oz. clear school glue
½ cup liquid starch
Water beads
Medium mixing bowl
Large mixing bowl
Mixing spoon

STEP 1: Gather supplies. Water beads are tiny beads made from plastic polymer that expand when exposed to moisture. You can find them online or at a local floral shop.

STEP 2: In a medium mixing bowl, pre-soak your water beads according to package directions.

STEP 3: Your water beads should be full size before making your slime. Drain any excess water from your mixing bowl. Set aside.

STEP 4: Pour 5 oz. clear school glue into large mixing bowl.

STEP 5: Add ½ cup liquid starch and stir until slime forms.

STEP 6: While slime is still setting, mix in by hand as many beads as you like. Let slime rest for 2-3 minutes before play.

BONUS PROJECT

OOBLECK

HERE'S WHAT YOU NEED:

1½ cup cornstarch
1 cup water
Medium mixing bowl
Mixing spoon
Food coloring

STEP 1: Gather supplies. Cornstarch can be found in most grocery stores in the baking aisle.

STEP 2: Pour 1 cup of water into a medium mixing bowl.

STEP 3: Slowly add cornstarch, one tablespoon at a time, until mixture starts to solidify.

STEP 4: Mix in food coloring.

STEP 5: Continue to slowly add cornstarch until mixture becomes difficult to stir.

STEP 6: Pour mixture out on a flat surface for play. Oobleck will transform back and forth from a solid to a liquid, so it is a lot of fun, and a lot of mess!